Word Whirls

Word Whirls

nd other shape poems

Compiled by John Foster

OXFORD
UNIVERSITY PRESS

OXFORD

UNIVERSITY PRESS

Great Clarendon Street, Oxford OX2 6DP

Oxford University Press is a department of the University of Oxford.
It furthers the University's objective of excellence in research, scholarship,
and education by publishing worldwide in

Oxford New York

Auckland Cape Town Dar es Salaam Hong Kong Karachi
Kuala Lumpur Madrid Melbourne Mexico City Nairobi
New Delhi Shanghai Taipei Toronto

With offices in

Argentina Austria Brazil Chile Czech Republic France Greece
Guatemala Hungary Italy Japan Poland Portugal Singapore
South Korea Switzerland Thailand Turkey Ukraine Vietnam

Oxford is a registered trade mark of Oxford University Press
in the UK and in certain other countries

This selection and arrangement copyright © John Foster 1998
Illustrations by Clare Hemstock

The moral rights of the author have been asserted

Database right Oxford University Press (maker)

First published 1998
First published in this edition 2005

British Library Cataloguing in Publication Data

Data available

ISBN-13: 978-0-19-279156-7
ISBN-10: 0-19-279156-7

1 3 5 7 9 10 8 6 4 2

Printed in Great Britain by
Cox & Wyman, Reading, Berkshire

Contents

Wrinkled Snarls and Paddle Paws

Sunshape, Skyscape

Food for Thought

Beware the Allivator

Word Smattering

Fun and Games

From Top to Toe

Steel, Stone, and Concrete

Word Whirls

On the wheel of words, words whirl, words swirl, words twist, words twirl. Inside the wheel of words, words dance, words prance, words spin, words grin. Words curl, words whirl.

John Foster

Wrinkled Snarls
and
Paddle Paws

Tall Talk

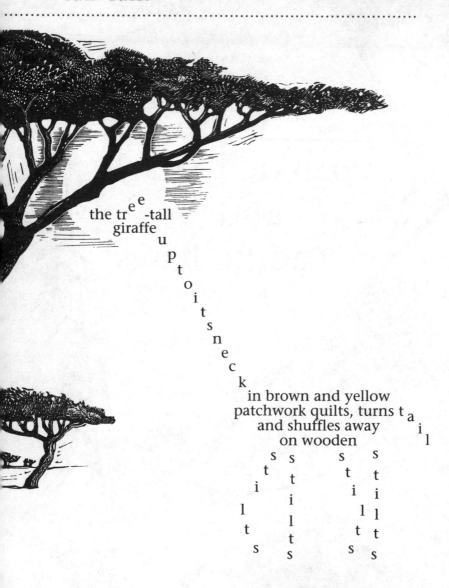

the tr^e^e-tall
giraffe
    u
     p
      t
       o
        i
         t
        s
       n
      e
     c
      k

in brown and yellow
patchwork quilts, turns t a
and shuffles away   i
on wooden   l

       s   s   s   s
        t   t   t   t
      i   i   i   i
      l   l   l   l
      t   t   t   t
      s   s   s   s

J. Patrick Lewis

Spider

trapping flies
a thousand eggs
spying eyes
SPIDER **S**pindle legs
SPIDER!

Trevor Millum

Doggerel

"WHAT A DOG!" MEANS UGLY. "WHAT A BITCH!" IS SPITEFUL. BUT WE DOGS BARK SMUGLY. FOR WHEN A CANINE'S FRIGHTFUL WE THINK "WHAT A PERSON!" AS OUR VERSION. DEROGATORY.

Jenny Morris

Mined by Moles

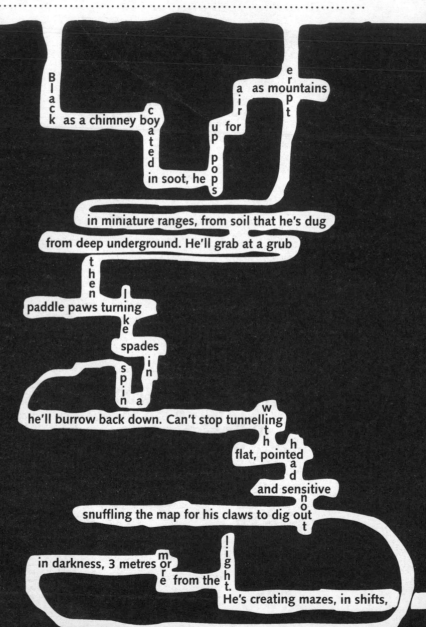

Black as a chimney boy

coated

in soot, he

up pops

air for

erupt

as mountains

in miniature ranges, from soil that he's dug

from deep underground. He'll grab at a grub

then

paddle paws turning

like

spades

in

spin

a

he'll burrow back down. Can't stop tunnelling

with

flat, pointed

head

and sensitive

not

snuffling the map for his claws to dig out

in darkness, 3 metres or more from the light.

He's creating mazes, in shifts,

**MINED
by
MOLES**

mound

high in this system of holes,

signed above ground by a

by being built h

cosily
naked and blind
curl in a
nest made of
grass where

avoids flood disaster

their nursery chamber

worms
and chasing earth
till this greed's satisfied
while little pink babies,

day and night,

Gina Douthwaite

17

Cat Dream

Catherine Benson

Blackbird

Black
bird.
Dead.
Dumped
in a bin. Your
life has been
taken. It seems
such a sin.
Did you fly at
a window that
mirrored the
tree? Not
everything
is what
it's
seen
to be.

Gina Douthwaite

Invasion

WITH THE FIRST EDGE OF LIGHT
THE GULLS CAME BEATING IN
FROM THE SEA
OVER

THE FARMLAND INTO ROOFCOUNTRY. DUST-
BIN COUNTRY, WAKING THE
TOWN

FROM ITS SUNDAY MORNING BED. THEY
FILLED THE AIR WITH THE
SCREAMS

OF THEIR DISSENSION, FILLED THE PALE
SKY WITH THEIR ARROGANT
STRONG

WINGS. WHEELING AND WEAVING THEY BUILT
A TOWERING PATTERN OF FLIGHT
ABOVE THE
TOWN.

Pamela Gillilan

Alphabirds

Ys owl

```
    YYY
    YYY
 YYYYYYY
 YYYYYYY
 Y  YYY  Y
    Y  Y
```

Cgull

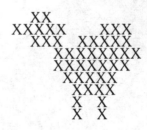

Pcock

```
    pppp
   pppppp
  pppppppp
 pppppppppp
    pppp
    pp
```

Chicken wire

```
      XX
  XXXXX      XXX
    XXX  XXXXX
       XXXXXXXX
       XXXXXXX
       XXXXX
       XXXX
       X  X
       X  X
```

Dave Calder

Sunshape,
Skyscape

Sunrise

h o r i z   n

     h o r i z O n

        h o r i z O n

          O
       h o r i z   n

Mike Johnson

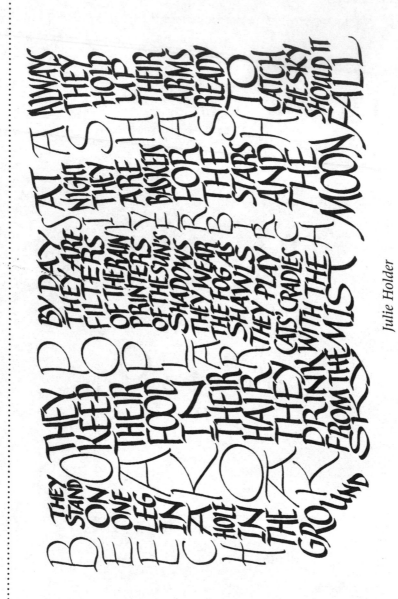

Julie Holder

Umbrella

Catherine Benson

Slowly slowly the leaves start to fall looks like autumn's decided to pay us a call

Tony Langham

Fire

FIRE

THAT WAVES THE FLAG OF

THE QUIET GHOST OF SMOKE

HIGHER

FURTHER

SPREADS

OF SMOKE

A WISPS

FOR

THEN THE FLAMES

THAT LICK A HOLE

IN THE DARK

THEN

THE

SPARK

FIRST THE KINDLING

Julie Holder

27

Winter

When sky unravels its cold myst-
eries

fluttering down brown skeletons of trees barely show

these speckles on a page can

the spectacle of un-expected snow

J. Patrick Lewis

Winter Walk

go.
to
like
would
we
where
show
snow
the
in
Footsteps

Patricia Leighton

Holiday Memories

IT WAS  COLD

AND I WAS FEELING REALY

AND  TO THE SKIN!

I REMEMBERED THE

HOLIDAY IN SPAIN—

 HOT WEATHER, CLEAR BLUE SEA,

 BEACHES AND A CLEAR SKY.

NOW IT'S ALL A MEMORY.

Paula Edwards

Snowdrop

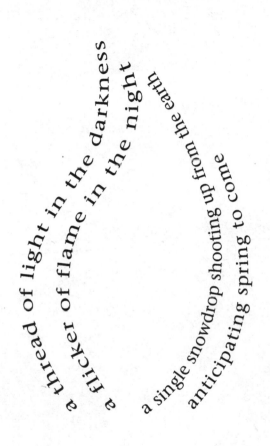

a thread of light in the darkness
a flicker of flame in the night
a single snowdrop shooting up from the earth
anticipating spring to come

Helena Hinn

Listen

Hear the spatter
Of the rain
Beat a rhythm
On the pane

Sending ripples through the puddles

Water rushing like a stream

Hear the anger of the rivers

Gushing torrents with a scream

As the motions of the oceans

Tremble, raging through the seas.

Maggie Holmes

Seahorses

Waves
and breakers
tumbling, ✱ rippling
across the sea,
smash them-
selves to
pieces, on
the shore,
in front of me.
When angry tempests
blow, wild horses
out of reach, plunge   and
toss snowy heads   and race
towards the beach.   White
crested seahorses,
prancing towards
the land.   Each
striving to
be first to
collapse
upon the
strand.
Seahor-
Janis Priestley   ses,
sea-
hor-
ses,
white
breakers
on the
sand.

33

Stone Haiku

Ground by cold rolling sea to smoothness, I fit now into your warm hand.

Hold me in your hand so your warmth can seep slowly into my cold heart.

Paper is flighty. But my calm gravity will keep it down to earth.

Put your ear to me: what will be ready to hatch if I crack open?

Michael Harrison

Food for
Thought

Breakfast

My daddy reads at breakfast,
We sometimes hear a mutter,
We wonder what he's up to
It must be fascinating, but
If one of us should ask him,
But Mummy says it's cricket,
Then when he folds his paper
His egg and toast are eaten,
So, when I need permission
I don't ask him at teatime
I wait until it's breakfast,
And if he mumbles 'Mmmm',

He holds THE TIMES up high.
And sometimes catch a sigh.
Behind that screen of print.
We've not the smallest hint.
He says it's 'world affairs',
Or boring stocks and shares.
And grabs his things to go,
Quite how, we'll never know.
For something I have planned,
—For then he'd understand—
Then make my special plea,
That's good enough for me!

Noel Petty

36

Sisters

sssssss
si
ssssss
ss
ssssssters sssss
sssssss
si
ssss
ssssssssssss
sssss
sters ssssssssss

Gina Douthwaite

Mirror rorriM

You looking out
at me looking in—
I am an **I**-
dentical twin!
Did I just wink?
I thought I did,
because you flut-
tered your eyelid.
When one of you
makes two of me
there's twice as much
of *us* to see!

tuo gnikool uoY
—ni gnikool em ta
-**I** na ma I
!niwt lacitned
?kniw tsuj I diD
,did I thguoht I
-tulf uoy esuaceb
.dileye ruoy deret
uoy fo eno nehW
em fo owt sekam
hcum sa eciwt s'ereht
!ees ot *us* fo

J. Patrick Lewis

Catherine Wheel

I used to go around with her all the time until we had this row and she went off with Tracy so that Tracy left me to tag along with Wendy and Debs till they stopped speaking to each other and I couldn't choose between them when up comes Anyusha who'd fallen out with her friend Jackie and we argued over who loved Gary Nunn most and Tracy emigrated so that was that and that's why I'm going round with Catherine AGAIN

David Horner

Lean cuisine
is not my scene...

FAT CUISINE,
CREAM CUISINE,
GREASY-SPOON-CANTEEN CUISINE
DON'T-SERVE-A-SPRAT
JUST-SERVE-A-SPRAT
CUISINE
TRIPLE-PORTION BEAN
CUISINE...
NEVER MIND
YOUR MEAN CUISINE
TRIFLE WITH ICE CREAM
CUISINE
IS SOMETHING MORE LIKE
MY CUISINE!

Judith Nicholls

Candy Bar

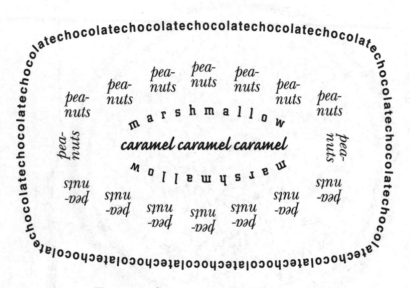

Too much.
Too much.
But I'll have one more.

Robert Froman

Spaghetti Poem

Forks are for twirling sp_ag_het_ti

But sometimes it slips straight t_ro_ug_h

If you find a strand t_ra_il_in_g

Suck s l o w l y — or failing

That, nip it in ha lf as you chew sp_ag_he_tt_i

Sue Cowling

Orange

I am a bright round orange

Quite sun-like in my beauty,

Peel off my skin
        and then you'll find

Me succulent and fruity.

John Cotton

Pineapple

My face may be rough
        and quite scaly,

And my hair's a bit like
        a punk's,

But inside I'm sweet
        and a bit of a treat,

With ice cream
        and cut up in chunks.

John Cotton

Drink Me!

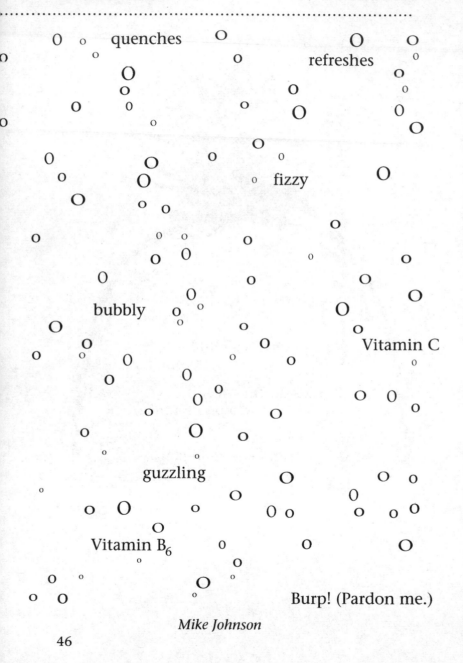

quenches

refreshes

fizzy

bubbly

Vitamin C

guzzling

Vitamin B_6

Burp! (Pardon me.)

Mike Johnson

Filtered Magic

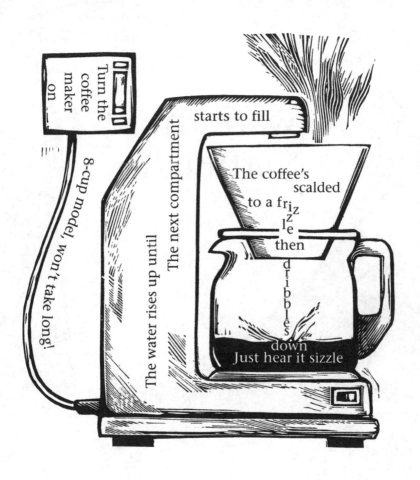

Turn the coffee maker on

8-cup model, won't take long!

The water rises up until

The next compartment

starts to fill

The coffee's
scalded
to a frizzle
then
dribbles
down
Just hear it sizzle

Trevor Harvey

Beware the
Allivator

The Allivator

at the top.

then eat you

his back

ride upon

let you

he will

in a shop

see one

if you

allivator

Beware the

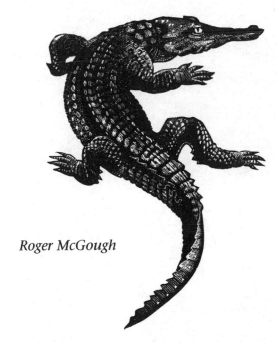

Roger McGough

The Claw

this is the
shape of the
monster's claw
glinting on its
massive paw
which quietly
opened the
bedroom door
and swung up
with one
terrible roar
over the bed
in the moon-
light before
it stabbed
into the
sleeper
to sil-
ence
his
snor
re
!

blood

d
r
i
p
p
e
d
down on the floor

Dave Calder

Creature

```
        I        am
      the    crazy
      crater creature,
    I creep across the
    crater 's    cracks
      and cr u nch the
        crimson crystals
          that cringe in
        crooked cul-de-sacs.
    Once a crumbling spacecraft crashed—
    an ancient cosmonaut crawled clear.
  Across the crinkled crust I chased her
    and chortling with churlish cheer
      caught        the        granny
      in             a          cranny
      of            the         crater
      and           ate          her
```

Dave Calder

Nessie

NESSiE rises from the depths of the still lake…

and beneath the dark dome of the watching sky

the endless ripples lace, lace, lace the water now.

Judith Nicholls

Corn Circle

WHO TRAMPLED IN THE CORN AND MADE AMAZING PATTERNS OVERNIGHT? IS IT A HOAX, OR DID SOME STRANGE SPACE-CRAFT APPEAR, AND HERE ALIGHT? WHAT WONDERFUL INTELLIGENCE HAS FOUND US OUT, AND LEFT THIS SIGN? AND WILL THEY ONE DAY DARE TO STAY, AND TALK WITH US, AND PROVE BENIGN?

Pam Gidney

53

Save the Smorkle Campaign

BUY SMORKLE FRIENDLY PRODUCTS HERE.

I ♥ MY SMORKLE —he's so cute!

WALK FOR SMORKLES Sponsor Form

IF YOU'VE HUGGED A SMORKLE—TOOT!

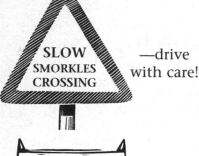

SLOW SMORKLES CROSSING —drive with care!

BAN SMORKLE HUNTING —it's not right!

Adopt-a-Smorkle Scheme. JOIN NOW.

SMORKLE SUPPORTERS' MARCH. UNITE!

Sue Cowling

54

The Twenty Steps to the Cellar

You descend with trepidation
one stone step at a time,
your torch illuminating
walls draped with 'webs and grime.
Down this same foot-worn stairway,
for centuries gone by,
tramped scullions and kitchen-maids,
came servants with a sigh
to dump unwanted chattels
by gleam of flick'ring lamp
on the cellar's cold flagstones
amidst the rising damp.
And now their shades surround you,
throng the sour-sweet air,
trailing shrouds of memories
that touch and wisp your hair,
but you must keep descending
a step, then one step more,
until at last you stand upon
the cellar's flagstoned floor.

Wes Magee

For Sale

Droves
of dry
r o t
creep-
ing up
from the
cellar,

back-biting winds whipping under the door,
Victorian corpse, skin candlewax yellow,
lies on a table-high bed where the floor
tilts like the deck of a ship on an ocean,
creaks as if speaking, glints red in a flicker
of lamplight that wanders in
strange floating motion, held in
the hand of some black-gaitered vicar
who passes through windows
both shuttered and barred, and chanting
winds buckets of blood from a well
that's strangled by yew trees
beside the churchyard.
To view: call the Devil on—666 Hell.

VICARAGE

Gina Douthwaite

Hallowe'en Hot-Pot

Blackhead of a greasy skin
in the cauldron simmering,
hair of nose and wax of ear,
scurf of scalp and salt of tear,
sticky eye and fur of tongue,
plaque of tooth and blood of gum.
For a spell stir at the double,
bring it to the boil
and bubble.

Gina Douthwaite

57

Word
Smattering

Word Smattering

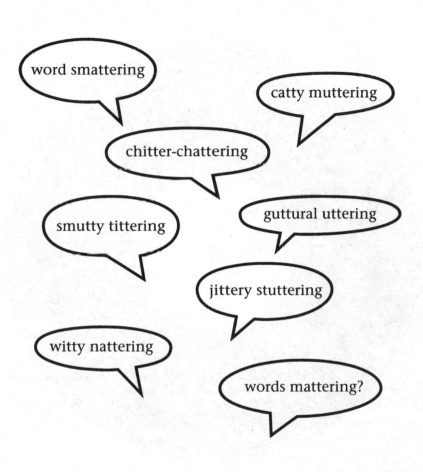

word smattering

catty muttering

chitter-chattering

smutty tittering

guttural uttering

jittery stuttering

witty nattering

words mattering?

Sue Cowling

Dizzy Dancer's Disco Party starts on Friday, 7.30, at the HITS and MISSES Club, Flip Side, Lyric. Please be good and send your answer promptly back to Dizzy Dancer — R.S.V.P.

R.S.V.P

Dizzy ● Dancer

45, Stylus,
GROOVYTRACK,
Charts.
TOP20 1CD

Gina Douthwaite

The Letter That Was Never Sent

THE LETTER THAT WAS NEVER SENT

WORDS YOU NEVER SAID

THE SENTIMENTS UNREAD

AND NOW, TOO LATE, ARE HID.

THE FEELINGS THAT YOU

MEANT TO STATE AND NEVER DID THE

Trevor Millum

Soft and *humming*—

LOUD

and *strumming*—

Listen to that **NEAT** refrain!

Add a **TRUMPET**

And a

 kit—

Why not change the B
E
    A
      T again?

UP
THE *VOLUME*

Eardrum priser,

 POP GROUP
SyntheSIZER!

Trevor Harvey

I AM THE PHONE THAT
RINGS   AND   RINGS
THE MESSAGE
LEFT UNANSWERED
I AM ALL THE CALLS
HEARD BLEEPING IN AN EMPTY
ROOM LIKE VOICES ENDLESSLY
REPEATING IN A TOMB...

Trevor Millum

Music

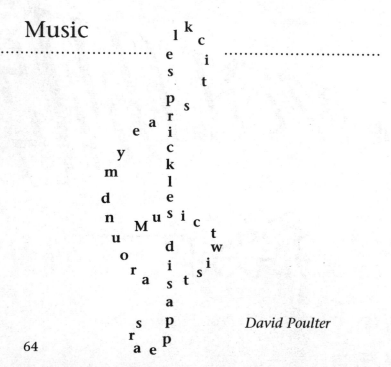

David Poulter

Fun and Games

Dive and Dip

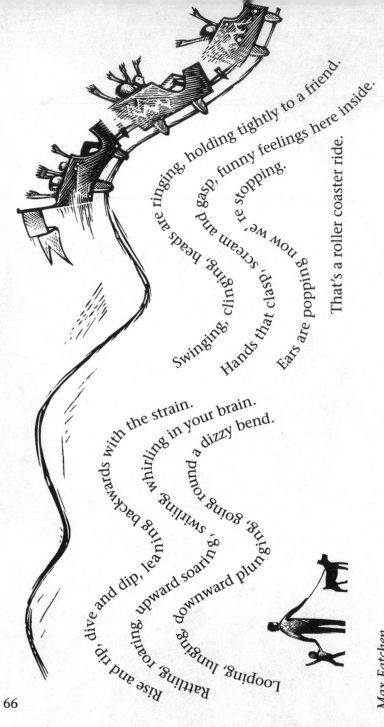

Rise and dip, dive and dip, leaning backwards with the strain.
Rattling, roaring, lunging, whirling in your brain.
Looping, upward soaring, swirling round a dizzy bend.
downward plunging, going round
Swinging, climbing, heads are ringing, holding tightly to a friend.
Hands that clasp, scream and gasp, funny feelings here inside.
Ears are popping now we're stopping.
That's a roller coaster ride.

Max Fatchen

Katherine Gallagher

KickingtheCircleKickingtheCircleKickingtheCircleKickingtheCircleKickingtheCircleKickingtheCircleKickingtheCircleKickingtheCircle

Football

How to Line Up Your Team

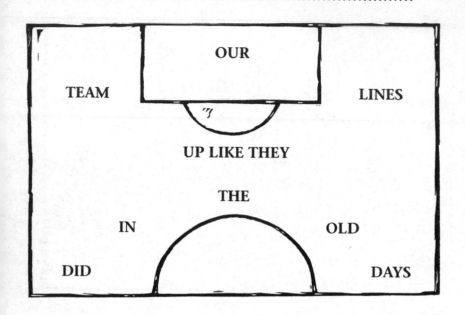

OUR

TEAM

LINES

UP LIKE THEY

THE

IN

OLD

DID

DAYS

FOR
THIS GAME WE ALL
CON CEN TRATE
ON DE FENCE

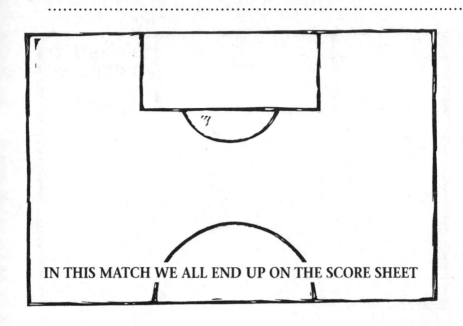

IN THIS MATCH WE ALL END UP ON THE SCORE SHEET

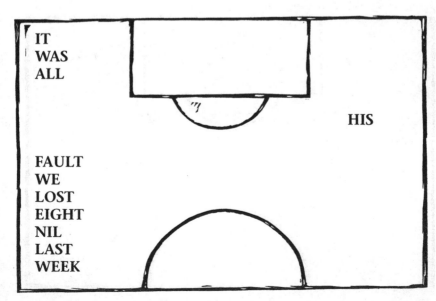

IT
WAS
ALL

HIS

FAULT
WE
LOST
EIGHT
NIL
LAST
WEEK

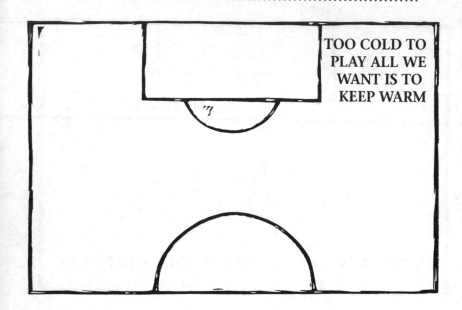

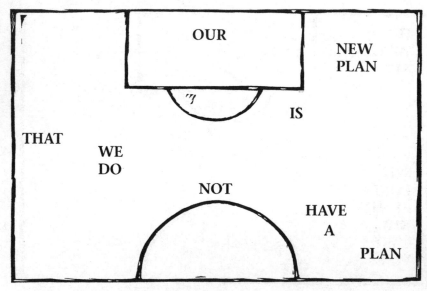

John Coldwell

Duck

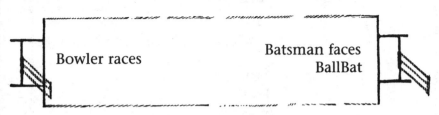

Bowler races   Batsman faces
                           BallBat

F
  i
   e
    l
     d
      e
       r
        c
         h
          a
           s
            e
              s   Howzatt!

Caught
For 0.

John Coldwell

DISMAL TEST MAKE ME RATTY. (SCORES) I'M A LITTLE (CRICKET BATTY)

Jenny Morris

Such a Racket

Whack crack,
There - - - - and - - - - back,
Whizzing to and fro.
Swinging swerving,
Sizzling *high* serving,
Hitting and low.
Lashing crashing,
Dashing smashing,
Hear the linesman's call.
Belted spun,
There's not much fun,
When you're a tennis ball.

Max Fatchen

Playtime

The thing is not to stand around or lean against the railings looking fed up on your own So what I do is I walk about the playground like I'm dead busy like I'm doing now then just before the whistle blows I've made myself a STAR

David Horner

Only a Game

```
          PRESS - - - Re diddlediddlediddle de de dee...
          GO! Karate Haiku Kid walkwalkwalkwalk
                                             STOP
          Warriors From The Gates Of Dawn    ATTACK
0                       K
                    C one f        y  y
            UM I      a          a   a   y
            J P K        I          r  r  a
              . .     I          p p   r
10          .  s  vanishes in a spray of pixels
                  .  *  .           p p
            P . / .              r    r  r
20          one EX   . *       ES        a    a  a
            L . . .            y         y   y

                   *    . — .
                        one gets chopped
                                        in ha
30                          lf & disapp....
       Re diddlediddle—BEEP!*BEEP!*BEEP!* – – – a blade  S
                                                          W
                                                           I
                                                          N
                                                        S G
                             d.g.
             in & Karate Haiku Kid d.o. e.s. OK OK OK walkwalk
40 walkwalkwalkwalk – but
                      WAIT it's the Black HOLE here with
out warning Karate Haiku Kid tries to NRUT but g r a v i t y
p u l l s  him  d o
                   w  n
                     .  .  .
```

Steve Bowkett

When You Walked Down the Passage

When you walked down the passage what did you see?

A DOOR WITH A MESSAGE THAT I KNEW WAS FOR ME

WHAT DID YOU FIND WHEN YOU OPENED THE DOOR?

I found a wooden chest in the middle of the floor—

what did you find when you opened the lid?

a parcel of paper sealed with wax that was red

what did you find when you op- ened the seal?

a picture of gran dad that was lifelike and real!

what did you see when you looked in his eyes?
a stare that went through me and saw through my lies

Trevor Millum

From Top
to Toe

Bodies are
blood, brains
and bones,
tubes that
loop
and
chromosomes,
organs, gastro-gases, guts, veins and valves,
and glands
with ducts,
fluids, flesh,
fat, feet,
and
fingers,
held in shape
(that's what the
skin does)

so
they
all
look
much
the
same.

That's
why
bodies
need
a
name.

Gina Douthwaite

Riddle Poem

my first is in hair
and also in hat

next   is in
EY   ES
&
also
in nose

my third is in laugh
but not in cries

my last
is   in
beard

but not   in toes

Trevor Millum

79

I

NEED

CONTACT

L E N S E S

like I need a poke in the eye

John Hegley

Who
knows
why a
nose has
hair? Don't
despair for
it's there
to deter
the entry of
dust which
turns to a crust,
clogs nostrils
and blocks off
t h e a i r

Gina Douthwaite

Belt

I am a belt. Thread me carefully around your waist and fasten me tight or I might let you down.

John Foster

Pants

the wind came roar
ing from the sea
it reeled around
respectable trees
it jigged   the roof
tiles up   and down
and knoc   ked old
ladies   to the
ground   ...but
worst,   in its
rough   panting
play   it dan
ced my   clean
pants   clean
                   away

Dave Calder

MY FIRST IS IN SOCK BUT NOT IN LOCKING. MY SECOND IN SHOCK BUT NOT IN STOCKING. MY THIRD IS IN BOOT AS WELL AS BROLLY. MY FOURTH IS IN WELLY BUT NOT IN WALLY.

Trevor Millum

Steel, Stone,
and Concrete

Pylons

```
                        P
                        Y
                        L
                        O
                        N
                        S

        tall                tall
       metal               steel
       trees                legs

              WE TALK

   no                           with
  birds   TO EACH OTHER         firm
  ever      CONSTANTLY          feet
  come                         planted

      MMMMmmmmmmmmmMMMM


nothing    OUR LINES CROSS AND HUM      we
comes      OUR ARMS OUTSTRETCHED       hum
 near        FINGERS FULL OF           over
  us          L I G H T N I N G        head


MMMMMMmmmmmmmmmmmmmmmmmMMMMMM

only       WE LINK CITIES AND SEAS TOGETHER     talk
 the           NO CHILDREN WILL PLAY             in
mist           NEAR US, NO ANIMALS             metal
comes                                          voices

      WE ARE SHUNNED AND FEARED BY EVERYONE

MMMMMMMMmmmmmmmmmmmmmmmmmmMMMMMMMM

  slowly      WE HAVE THE POWER TO          stiff
  coils     MAKE THE WORLD GO BLACK         grey
   our      TO CLOSE DOWN THE SYSTEM       strong
   toes        OF THE PLANET EARTH         things
 of power                                 of power
 of power                                 of power
 of power                                 of power
 of power                                 of power
MMMMMMMMMM                              MMMMMMMMMM
```

Christine Morton

Skyscrapers

L
L
A
T
LY
IB
RED
INC
ARE
PERS
SCRA
SKY-
SOME

L
AL
SM
TE
QUI
ARE
SOME

SKY?
THE
PE
RA
SC
TO
ED
NE
WE
DO
WHY
KNOW IS
I WANT TO
BUT WHAT

Tony Langham

The Bridge

Andrew Collett

```
            P
          E A K
        P L A C E
      P R O U D L Y
     P R O V I D I N G
   P R E S T I G I O U S
  P L U S H   P R I V A T E
  P I L E D   P E N T H O U S E
P E R F E C T L Y   P L A N N E D
P A N O R A M I C   P O S I T I O N
PART  PAYMENT  POSSIBLE
PAST PHARAOHS PREFERRED
```

Dave Calder

Weekend in the Country

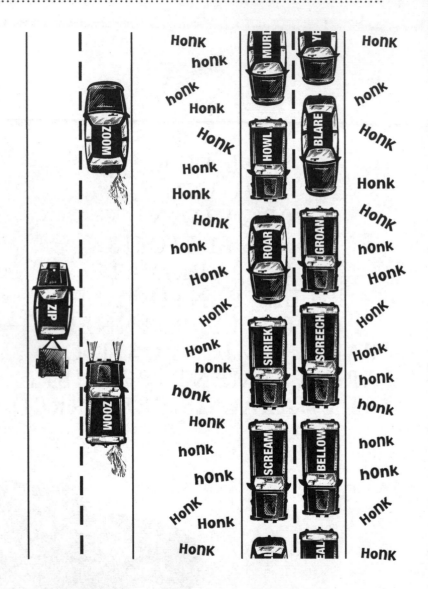

Robert Froman

The Concrete Poem

What is a concrete poem?
It doesn't sound quite right,
For concrete's rather heavy
And words are rather light.

Let's say you write a poem—
'Ode to a concrete slab'—
A subject none too pretty,
Which many would call drab.
Perhaps you could describe it
As full of strength and grace
And muse on what high tower
Might rest upon that base.
You may contrast its texture
With wood and weathered stone
And wonder if it will some day
Be mellowed, creeper-grown.

But if you set the words out
And shape your poem, too,
To be the slab's three faces
With each face seen askew,
So that the poem's reader
Can look as well as hear,
Why then, your final poem
Is Concrete—is that clear?

Noel Petty

Index of titles and first lines

First lines are in italic

Index of authors

Acknowledgements

The editor and publisher are grateful for permission to include the following poems:

Catherine Benson: 'Cat Dream' and 'Autumn', both Copyright © Catherine Benson 1998, first published in this collection by permission of the author. **Steve Bowkett**: 'Only a Game', first published in Trevor Harvey (ed.): *Techno Talk (poems with byte)* (Bodley Head, 1994), reprinted by permission of the author. **Dave Calder**: 'Snake's Dance' from *Bamboozled* (Other Publications, 1987); 'Alphabirds', 'The Claw', 'Creature', 'Pants', and 'Pyramid', all Copyright © Dave Calder 1998, first published in this collection, all by permission of the author. **John Coldwell**: 'How to Line Up Your Team' first published in David Orme (ed.): *You'll Never Walk Alone* (Macmillan, 1995); 'Duck', Copyright © John Coldwell 1998, first published in this collection, both by permission of the author. **Andrew Collett**: 'The Bridge', Copyright © Andrew Collett 1998, first published in this collection by permission of the author. **John Cotton**: 'Orange' and 'Pineapple', both Copyright © John Cotton 1998, first published in this collection by permission of the author. **Sue Cowling**: 'Spaghetti Poem', 'Save the Smorkle Campaign', and 'Word Smattering', all Copyright © Sue Cowling 1998, first published in this collection by permission of the author. **Gina Douthwaite**: 'Sisters' and 'Dizzy Dancer's Disco Party Invitation' from *Picture a Poem* (Hutchinson, 1994), Copyright © Gina Douthwaite 1994; 'Blow This', first published in *Nothing Tastes Quite Like a Gerbil* (Macmillan, 1996), Copyright © Gina Douthwaite 1996, 'Mined by Moles', 'Blackbird', 'For Sale', 'Hallowe'en Hot-Pot', and 'Bodies', all Copyright © Gina Douthwaite 1998, first published in this collection, all by permission of the author. **Paula Edwards**: 'Holiday Memories', first published in Gervase Phinn (ed.): *Lizard Over Ice* (Nelson), reprinted by permission of Gervase Phinn. **Max Fatchen**: 'Dive and Dip' and 'Such a Racket', from *Peculiar Rhymes and Lunatic Lines* (first published in the UK by Orchard Books, a division of the Watts Publishing Group, 96 Leonard Street, London EC2A 4RH, reprinted by permission of the publishers. **John Foster**: 'Word Whirls' and 'Belt', Copyright © John Foster 1998, first published in this collection by permission of the author. **Robert Froman**: 'Candy Bar' (originally entitled 'Well, Yes') from *Street Poems* (McCall Pub. Co., 1971) and 'A Weekend in the Country' from *Seeing Things* (T. Crowell, 1974), reprinted by permission of Katherine Froman. **Katherine Gallagher**: 'Football', Copyright © Katherine Gallagher 1998, first published in this collection by permission of the author. **Pam Gidney**: 'Corn Circle', Copyright © Pam Gidney 1998, first published in this collection by permission of the author. **Pamela Gillilan**: 'Invasion', first published in John Foster (ed.) *A Fifth Poetry Book* (OUP, 1985), Copyright © Pamela Gillilan 1985, reprinted by permission of the author. **Michael Harrison**: 'Stone Haiku' from *Junk Mail* (OUP, 1993), reprinted by permission of the author. **Trevor**